Before You Give Up

A 7-Day Devotional

ELIZABETH WILSON

Nova Sei
PRESS

Before You Give Up
A 7-Day Devotional
Seeds of Significance: Book 1

Copyright © 2026 by Elizabeth Wilson
All rights reserved.

Published by Nova Sei Press
Tennessee, USA | www.novaseipress.com

Printed in the United States of America

ISBN: 979-8-9946788-4-8

Welcome to your "back of the boat." Jesus lived like this, and so can you.

INTRODUCTION

Most of us can relate to this fork in the road: Do I give up or press through?

Sometimes, all we really need is a snack or a nap, and after that, the moment passes. Other times, though, we are facing a decision that matters. One that could affect our time, our energy, our capacity, and sometimes the people around us.

Before we give up anything, let's make sure we're letting go of the things that don't belong in our lives.

This devotional is here to help you navigate that question, not just once, but any time you encounter it. Consider these pages a mini blueprint, a guided return to peace in your heart and confidence in your next steps. This may look like either fresh strength to continue on your current path, or courage to step onto a better one.

Do you remember when Jesus and His disciples were crossing the sea, and He told them they were going to the other side? He went to the back of the boat to take a nap, and He was still fast asleep when the disciples rushed to wake Him for fear of their lives. Jesus was unworried, at total peace.

Welcome to your "back of the boat." Jesus lived like this, and so can you.

On the same day, when evening had come, He said to them, "Let us cross over to the other side." Now when they had left the multitude, they took Him along in the boat as He was. And other little boats were also with Him. And a great windstorm arose, and the waves beat into the boat, so that it was already filling. But He was in the stern, asleep on a pillow. And they awoke Him and said to Him, "Teacher, do You not care that we are perishing?"

Then He arose and rebuked the wind, and said to the sea, "Peace, be still!" And the wind ceased and there was a great calm. But He said to them, "Why are you so fearful? How is it that you have no faith?"

MARK 4:35–40

Rushing to react
is rarely as helpful as
pausing to reflect.

DAY ONE

Why Are You Tired?

Wouldn't it be great if we could manage our sleep perfectly, never feel overwhelmed in our daily life, and always budget our time and money without error? Although that may be a refreshing thought, it's not realistic. There are many things outside our control in our daily lives.

When we feel like we're running on empty, something caused that. Maybe it's what we're doing. Maybe it's how we're doing it. Maybe it's a timing issue. Are we rushing something? Are we sitting on it longer than we should? Should we not be doing it at all?

One thing is certain: rushing to react is rarely as helpful as pausing to reflect. Today is about beginning that reflection so we can choose how to respond.

When we react quickly, it's often out of stress, frustration, or uncomfortable emotions like anxiety or embarrassment. Taking time to reflect allows us to respond intentionally, from a steadier and less emotional place.

> A fool vents all his feelings, but a wise man holds them back.
> —Proverbs 29:11

This verse has corrected me more times than I can count, and I'm thankful for it. It is a life-giving Word that invites self-control and discipline, especially when emotions are running high.

It can be all too easy to let everything spill out when we're worn down, but this scripture reminds us that wisdom often looks like restraint. Many of us can likely attest to how destructive a lack of restraint can be.

> Whoever guards his mouth and tongue keeps his soul from troubles.
> —Proverbs 21:23

One thing that certainly requires protection

and discipline is our soul. Our soul is made up of our mind, will, and emotions. When these are left unguarded, they can pull us to act from our flesh rather than our spirit.

> The spirit indeed is willing, but the flesh is weak.
>
> —MATTHEW 26:41B

As we diligently guard our thoughts and emotions, our mouth (what we say) is also being guarded. The result is our will being better positioned to yield to God's direction. This becomes especially important when we feel worn down and tempted to give up.

TODAY'S REFLECTION QUESTIONS:
1. What is one thing you sense is draining or depleting you right now?
2. Why do you think it is having that effect?

He is with us,
and He is with us
strong. He is our
very present help.

DAY TWO

What's Your Next Move?

Now that you've identified something that's wearing on you, it's time to decide what to do about it. Do you need refreshing to manage it, or do you need courage to release it?

> If any of you lacks wisdom, let him ask of God, who gives to all liberally and without reproach, and it will be given to him.
> —JAMES 1:5

Take a moment to ask God for His wisdom in your situation. Ask Him to show you clearly what you need and what your next steps are.

> God is our refuge and strength, a very present help in trouble.
>
> —PSALM 46:1

When we approach the Lord in faith, we can rest assured that His help is available to us because His Word has already promised it. He is not reluctant to help. He is eager. He loves us deeply.

At this crossroads in your life, do you need more of Him to sustain you through this season? Or do you need more of Him to courageously release something that does not belong in your life?

Whichever direction you sense today, the first step is the same. Take time with the Lord. Invite His presence, and allow Him to fill you with His goodness, His strength, His peace, and His joy. Spend time thanking Him for where He has brought you from, how faithful He has been, the truth of His Word at work in your life, the people He has placed around you, and even the small blessings that may often go unnoticed.

The Lord's rivers of living water flow into our lives to refresh the soil of our heart and quench the thirst of our soul and spirit. He is with us, and He is with us *strong*. He is our very present help.

TODAY'S REFLECTION QUESTIONS:
1. Are you allowing the Lord's rivers of living water to flow in your life?
2. Is there an area where you sense He wants to bring greater refreshing? If so, ask Him. He loves you and will help you.

Over time, something
meant to be a
blessing can quietly
become a substitute.

DAY THREE

Where Do You Find Peace?

There is nowhere we can go that compares to the presence of the Lord. Many of us know this, yet we may not choose His presence when we are feeling troubled or tired.

When we are seeking peace for our hearts, where do we turn first? Do we reach for books or television, or do we draw near to the presence of God? There are many helpful resources and people in our lives, and these can be precious blessings from the Lord. But does He hold *first place* in our hearts, above every blessing He has given us?

You shall have no other gods before Me.
—Exodus 20:3

Other gods are not limited to physical idols held in our hands. An idol is anything that takes a higher place in our hearts than God. This can happen subtly, even with good things. It may be a job, an assignment the Lord has given us, a relationship, our home, or a hobby. Over time, something meant to be a blessing can quietly become a substitute.

> Jesus said to him, "You shall love the Lord your God with all your heart, with all your soul, and with all your mind. This is the first and great commandment."
> —Matthew 22:37–38

When the Lord truly holds first place, no lesser source of peace will satisfy us. We choose Him, and we choose His presence. He is the foundation and source of our peace. Everything else is meant to support and complement that peace, not compete with it.

This is the same peace Jesus rested with in the back of the boat, even as a storm raged all around Him. When He was awakened by His panicked disciples, His peace still didn't waver. This is the peace we can rest in, day and night. It is the peace we make right decisions from, steady and aligned with God's plan for us.

TODAY'S REFLECTION QUESTIONS:
1. Where is the first place you turn to when you are seeking peace?
2. Is spending time in the Lord's presence a daily practice that shapes where your heart runs when you are weary?

Is He our
everything,
or our
afterthought?

DAY FOUR

Who Touches Your Heart Most?

We have established our need for God's wisdom, presence, and peace in our daily lives. This is a trustworthy foundation we have begun building. Today, we shift our focus to our emotions. Without acknowledging and being intentional about them, we may experience disunity within ourselves.

> And if a house is divided against itself, that house cannot stand.
>
> —Mark 3:25

We are meant to live in unity—spirit, soul,

and body. At times, the most resistant part of us is our soul, which is made up of our mind, will, and emotions. This is why the Lord cares deeply about the condition of our soul. He calls and compels us to have a *prosperous* soul.

> Beloved, I pray that you may prosper in all things and be in health, just as your soul prospers.
>
> —3 JOHN 2

Where do we seek affection and comfort? Do we look first to people, or to the Lord? Is He our everything, or our afterthought? We have already seen His promise to be our very present help. Do we run to Him when we are tired, hurt, startled, or afraid?

When someone delivers difficult news, or circumstances feel heavy or uncertain, do we press into God's Word for truth and comfort? Do we allow His presence to steady our hearts and realign us with His will and plan?

Is our most sought-after affection and comfort found in the Lord, or in people or something else? There is no wound He cannot heal, no brokenness He cannot restore, and no question He does not already hold the answer to.

> But God demonstrates His own love toward us, in that while we were still sinners, Christ died for us.
>
> —ROMANS 5:8

Oh, how He loves us! Jesus' obedience to the Father's will led Him to the cross, where He endured tremendous suffering for the joy set before Him: *us*. He conquered death and Hell, ascended to Heaven, and even now sits at the right hand of the Father, interceding for you and for me.

Today and every day, the Lord invites you to receive His affection, comfort, and help.

TODAY'S REFLECTION QUESTIONS:

1. Who touches your heart most when it cries out for comfort and affection?
2. Is there something heavy on your heart that you need to invite the Lord to heal or help you release? If so, ask Him now.

True joy comes
from the throne
room of Heaven.

DAY FIVE

When Did You Last
Take Your Medicine?

Today, we're going both lighter and deeper at the same time. We're looking at one of the Bible's primary prescriptions for our daily lives: the joy of the Lord. This lightens our load significantly, and to understand and apply it properly, we're digging deeper into the Word.

> A merry heart does good, like medicine,
> —Proverbs 17:22a

The Hebrew word translated "merry" in this scripture is *sameach*, which describes "a state of settled gladness that springs from covenant favor, obedience, and God-given blessing. Unlike fleeting amusement, the adjective regularly portrays joy that is morally congruent with the character and purposes of the Lord. It is often paired with worship terms or covenant celebrations, signaling that true gladness is rooted in relationship with God."[1]

This merry heart refers to a heart overflowing with the joy of the Lord, which makes sense because Scripture also tells us:

> Do not sorrow, for the joy of the Lord is
> your strength.
> —NEHEMIAH 8:10B

True joy comes from the throne room of Heaven. It strengthens us and gives us access to what the Lord desires to do in and through our lives.

> Therefore with joy you will draw water
> from the wells of salvation.
> —ISAIAH 12:3

---

1. BibleHub, s.v. "Strong's Hebrew 8056. חָמֵשׂ (sameach) — Joyful, glad, merry, happy," accessed February 4, 2026, https://biblehub.com/hebrew/8056.htm.

The Hebrew word translated "salvation" in this verse, *yeshuah*, "gathers the ideas of rescue, deliverance, help, victory, and the well-being that follows divine intervention."[2] These wells of salvation contain everything we need, and Scripture tells us that joy is the bucket which draws from them.

Joy is not a small thing. It is a vital and precious gift from the Lord, meant to strengthen our hearts and steady our lives as we walk with Him. Through His joy, we hold the key to every victory and provision.

TODAY'S REFLECTION QUESTIONS:

1. When you spend time in the presence of God, do you intentionally allow your heart to enter into His joy?
2. Has the joy of the Lord been a steady pillar in your life? Do you desire to experience His joy to a greater level than you have before?

---

2. BibleHub, s.v. "Strong's Hebrew 3444. הָעוֹשִׁי (yeshuah) — Salvation, deliverance, victory," accessed February 4, 2026, https://biblehub.com/hebrew/3444.htm.

You and God
form a majority,
every time!

DAY SIX

Whose Report Do You Believe?

Today, we're asking ourselves a question that gives us precise coordinates for our intended destination: Whose report do you believe?

> God is not a man, that He should lie, nor a son of man, that He should repent. Has He said, and will He not do? Or has He spoken, and will He not make it good?
> —Numbers 23:19

Everything God says is true. Anything spoken in contradiction to the Word of God, while possibly a natural fact, is a lie that is in opposition to the truth of God's Word. When we take the truth of God's Word and declare it in faith over our situation, we team up with God Himself to turn the tide of our circumstance. Even natural facts must bow to the authority of God's Word when we declare it in faith. They are not set in stone just because they present themselves.

> And they went out and preached everywhere, the Lord working with them and confirming the word through the accompanying signs. Amen.
>
> —MARK 16:20

As the disciples went forth proclaiming God's Word, He confirmed His Word with accompanying miracles. How do we know He will always do this?

> So shall My word be that goes forth from My mouth; it shall not return to Me void, but it shall accomplish what I please, and it shall prosper in the thing for which I sent it.
>
> —ISAIAH 55:11

You and God form a majority, every time! No matter what diagnosis a doctor states, which doors close suddenly, when discouragement or criticism comes, or a storm rages—we *cannot* be defeated or overcome if we choose to believe the report of the Lord.

> What then shall we say to these things? If
> God is for us, who can be against us?
> —ROMANS 8:31

The key to living undefeated is to receive and believe the Word of God, declaring it from our mouth and letting it form deep roots in our heart.

TODAY'S REFLECTION QUESTIONS:
1. Do you know what God's Word says about you and your situation?
2. Are you equipped with scriptures to stand on in faith to turn the tide of your circumstance?

The "back of the boat"
isn't just a place
we visit. It's a posture
we live with.

DAY SEVEN

Will You Make Room?

Here we are at Day 7. We are making great progress in the span of just one week. Today, we're considering what we may have in our lives that doesn't belong, so that we can position ourselves to release it. When we release the wrong things, we make room for the right things. Are you ready to lighten your load?

On Day 1, we looked at what might be depleting us and why it feels like that.

On Day 2, we established the importance of spending time with God in His presence, and that it's the first step toward determining our next steps.

On Days 3 and 4, we examined our heart and our

habits or inclinations.

On Day 5, we focused on joy as a powerful biblical prescription for accessing God's provision and strength.

On Day 6, we contrasted the truth of God's Word with every potential opposition, unlocking a key to victory.

Today, we reflect on each of the truths and teachings we've encountered together this week. Today, we decide what we're going to do. Is this going to be just information we've learned, or are we going to allow these things to spark transformation within us and throughout our lives?

> But be doers of the word, and not hearers
> only, deceiving yourselves.
> —JAMES 1:22

As doers of the Word, we're going to put into practice these things we have learned.

> Your word is a lamp to my feet and a light
> to my path.
> —PSALM 119:105

This week, we've been hearing what God has to say. His Word is speaking directly to us, lighting our path and showing us the way. Now it's our decision to walk in it—not just once, but every day. Now we build upon this foundation with daily faithfulness and obedience.

Each time we find ourselves at a crossroads, faced with the decision to sustain or release, these same principles apply. The specifics come from the Lord as we invite Him to speak to us.

The "back of the boat" isn't just a place we visit. It's a posture we live with.

TODAY'S REFLECTION QUESTIONS:
1. Do you desire more of what God has for you and your life?
2. Are you willing to release what's holding you back, so that you can receive God's best for you?

A life wholly surrendered
to God is the key to
living victoriously from
God's strength.

CONTINUE THE JOURNEY

If *Before You Give Up* encouraged you, you're invited to continue with *Just Give Up! When Striving Gives Way to God's Strength*.

A life wholly surrendered to God is the key to living victoriously from God's strength. You will face crossroads at different times, and there may even be times it seems there's no way through. Trust in God.

> …I will even make a road in the wilderness and rivers in the desert.
>
> —Isaiah 43:19

> The Lord is my strength and my shield; my heart trusted in Him, and I am helped; therefore my heart greatly rejoices, and with my song I will praise Him.
>
> —Psalm 28:7

NOTES

NOTES

NOTES

NOTES

POSTSCRIPT

It has been a pleasure to navigate this week with you in *Before You Give Up*, looking to God and His Word for truths you can apply to every situation you face. He is with you and for you; He has promised to never leave you or forsake you, but rather to be your very present help in time of need.

If this book has blessed you, you can contact us at novaseipress.com to share your testimony. We'd love to hear from and rejoice with you.

If you desire to see others find these seven days of simple but significant seeds of faith, you can write a review on Amazon or Goodreads, send a copy of this book to someone, or share about your experience on social media.

Lastly, if you'd like to continue this journey, join me for a deeper dive with my book, *Just Give Up! When Striving Gives Way to God's Strength*. I would love to share the rest of this message with you, imparting what I've learned, so that you have access to these keys the Lord has given me. What He has done for one, He will do for all. He is faithful.

Thank you for being here. I pray these pages transform your life beyond what you could have asked, thought, or imagined, as you apply the teachings within.

ABOUT THE AUTHOR

Elizabeth Wilson is the founder of Nova Sei Press, a publishing house committed to releasing Christian-authored books with excellence and helping self-publishing writers bring their projects to life with clarity and care. She studied at River University in Tampa, Florida, where her love for Scripture and ministry deepened.

Elizabeth lives in Tennessee with her husband and daughter. Her writing reflects her heart to encourage believers to live surrendered, rooted in truth, and confident in God's strength.

Connect with Elizabeth Wilson:

Instagram: @elizabethwilsonauthor

Facebook: @elizabethwilsonauthor.nsp

Goodreads: goodreads.com/elizabethwilsonauthor

Amazon: amazon.com/author/elizabethwilson-nsp

NOVA SEI PRESS

Nova Sei Press exists to publish Christian-authored books with excellence and to support independent authors through thoughtful, professional publishing services. With a focus on integrity, craftsmanship, and faithfulness to Scripture, Nova Sei Press seeks to steward words that strengthen the Church and serve readers well.

Connect with Nova Sei Press on Instagram, Facebook, and YouTube: @novaseipress.

Books by Elizabeth Wilson:

Before You Give Up: A 7-Day Devotional

Just Give Up! When Striving Gives Way to God's Strength

The Joyful Mother Promise: A 7-Day Devotional

Called to Motherhood: Trusting God Beyond Fear, Grief, and Delay

SEEDS OF SIGNIFICANCE

Seeds of Significance is a series of seven-day devotionals designed to plant biblical truth in everyday life. Each book offers short, Scripture-centered readings that take about five minutes a day, making it simple to stay rooted in God's Word even in a full season of life. This volume is the second in the series.

The Joyful Mother Promise, the second volume, establishes women in the Word for conception, pregnancy, and childbirth—no matter what natural facts may say.

The next volume in the series, *Gather Not A Few*, stirs up your faith expectation for God to do what He said He would do.

SALVATION

As you have been reading this book, maybe the Lord has been tugging at your heart in light of eternity. Yes, we have this life to live on the Earth, but then the Lord's plan is for Heaven to be our home in eternity, not the devil's Hell.

If you fit into any of the three categories below, I'm inviting you to pray now.
- You don't know for sure if you are on your way to Heaven.
- You haven't received Jesus into your heart as your personal Lord and Savior.
- You want to make a fresh commitment to the Lord and be confident that you are in right standing with Him.

Pray this prayer, and mean it in your heart as you speak the words out loud:

Father, I come to You in the precious Name of Your Son, Jesus. You said in Your Word, if I confess with my mouth and believe in my heart, that I will be saved. Forgive me of my sins. Wash me and cleanse me. Set me free. Jesus, I believe that You're risen from the dead, and You're coming back again for me. I forgive anyone who has ever hurt me, and I forgive myself. I'm saved, I'm born again, I'm forgiven, and I'm set free. Thank You, Lord, for saving me now. Give me a passion for the lost, a hunger for the things of God, and a holy boldness to preach the Gospel of Jesus Christ. I love You, Lord. In Jesus' Name, I pray. Amen.

As a minister of the Gospel of Jesus Christ, I tell you today that your sins are forgiven you right now. Always remember to run to God and not from Him, because He loves you and has a wonderful plan for your life.

9 798994 678848